APR 1 3

MARYLAND

Pamela McDowell

LET'S READ
AV²
BY WEIGL™
ADDED VALUE • AUDIO VISUAL

Go to **www.av2books.com**, and enter this book's unique code.

BOOK CODE

J227405

AV² by Weigl brings you media enhanced books that support active learning.

AV² provides enriched content that supplements and complements this book. Weigl's AV² books strive to create inspired learning and engage young minds in a total learning experience.

Your AV² Media Enhanced books come alive with...

Audio
Listen to sections of the book read aloud.

Video
Watch informative video clips.

Embedded Weblinks
Gain additional information for research.

Try This!
Complete activities and hands-on experiments.

Key Words
Study vocabulary, and complete a matching word activity.

Quizzes
Test your knowledge.

Slide Show
View images and captions, and prepare a presentation.

... and much, much more!

Published by AV² by Weigl
350 5th Avenue, 59th Floor
New York, NY 10118
Website: www.av2books.com   www.weigl.com

Library of Congress Cataloging-in-Publication Data
McDowell, Pamela.
 Maryland / Pamela McDowell.
    p. cm. -- (Explore the U.S.A.)
Includes bibliographical references and index.
ISBN 978-1-61913-359-4 (hard cover : alk. paper)
1. Maryland--Juvenile literature. I. Title.
F181.3.M39 2012
975.2--dc23
                          2012015076

Printed in the United States of America in North Mankato, Minnesota
1 2 3 4 5 6 7 8 9 16 15 14 13 12

052012
WEP040512

Project Coordinator: Karen Durrie
Art Director: Terry Paulhus

Weigl acknowledges Getty Images as the primary image supplier for this title.

MARYLAND

Contents

3

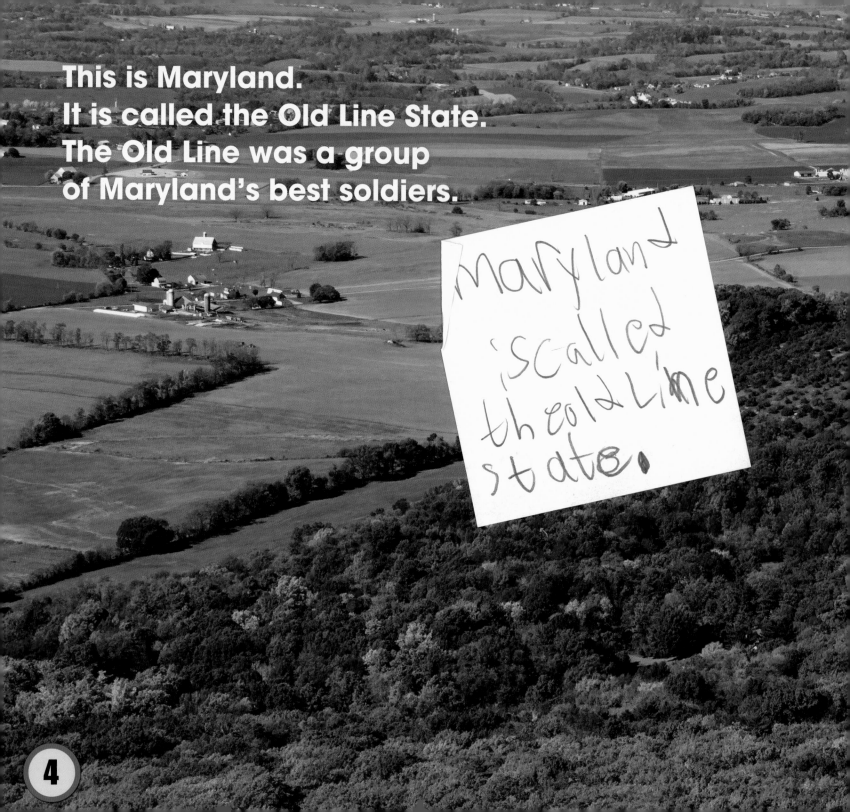

This is Maryland.
It is called the Old Line State.
The Old Line was a group
of Maryland's best soldiers.

Maryland
'scalled
theold Line
state.

This is the shape of Maryland. It is in the east part of the United States. Four states border Maryland.

maryland is rict thaer ↓

Where

Pacific Ocean

United States

Atlantic Ocean

Mexico

Maryland is next to the Atlantic Ocean.

The Star Spangled Banner was written in Maryland. It is the national anthem of the United States.

The Star Spangled Banner was written during a battle.

The black-eyed susan is the state flower of Maryland. It can grow up to six feet tall.

The Maryland state seal has two men and a crown.

The man on the left is a miner. The man on the right is a fisherman.

This is the state flag of Maryland. It is red, white, black, and gold.

The patterns on the flag come from two old Maryland families.

this is
← the state
flag

The Baltimore oriole is the state bird of Maryland. It eats insects, fruit, and nectar.

The Baltimore oriole makes two sounds when it whistles.

This is the state capital of Maryland. It is a city named Annapolis.

The United States Naval Academy is in Annapolis.

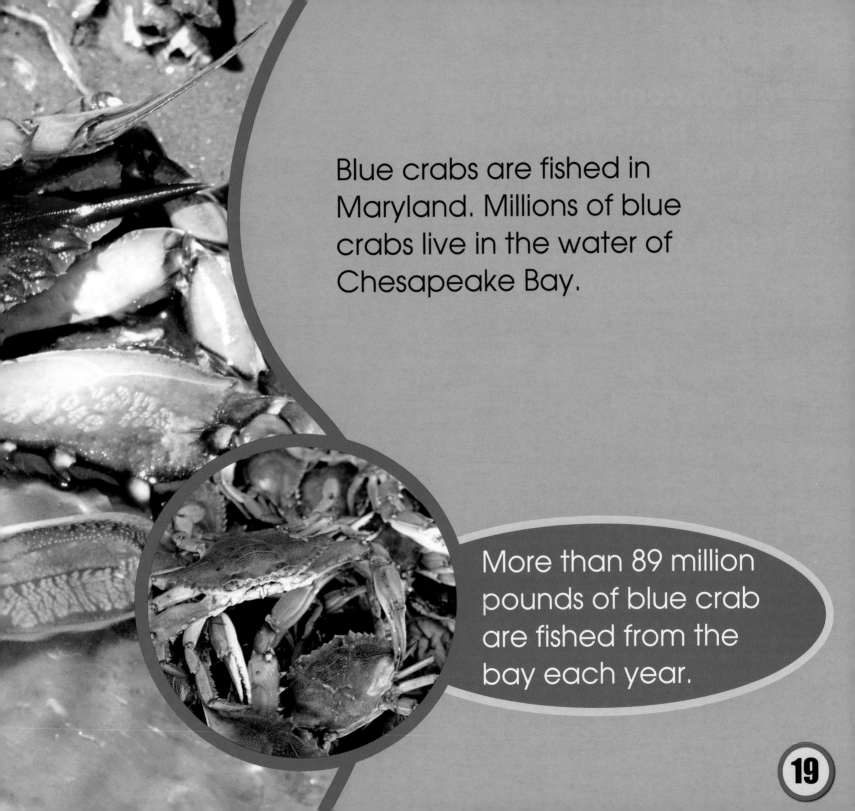

Blue crabs are fished in Maryland. Millions of blue crabs live in the water of Chesapeake Bay.

More than 89 million pounds of blue crab are fished from the bay each year.

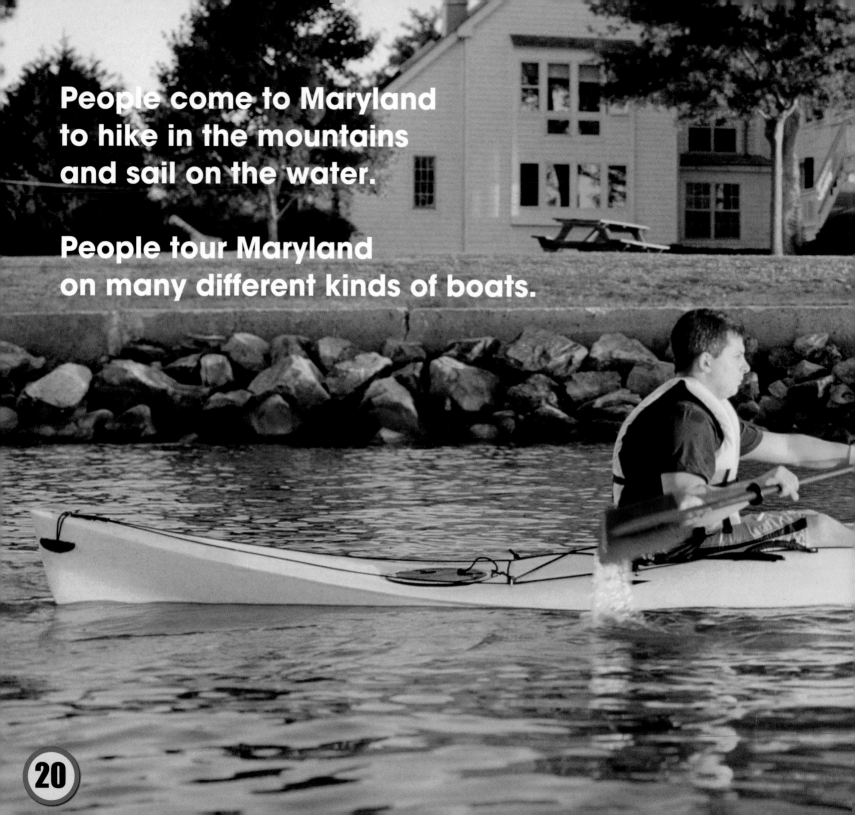

People come to Maryland
to hike in the mountains
and sail on the water.

People tour Maryland
on many different kinds of boats.

MARYLAND FACTS

These pages provide detailed information that expands on the interesting facts found in the book. These pages are intended to be used by adults as a learning support to help young readers round out their knowledge of each state in the *Explore the U.S.A.* series.

Pages 4–5

Maryland was one of the original 13 colonies. During the fight for independence, Maryland troops were rarely beaten in battle. The soldiers were called the "Maryland Line." President George Washington called these soldiers "The Old Line."

Pages 6–7

On April 28, 1788, Maryland became the seventh state to join the United States. Maryland is on the east coast of the United States. It is bordered by Pennsylvania to the north and Delaware to the east. West Virginia and Virginia are to the west of Maryland. The District of Columbia, or Washington, D.C., is surrounded by Maryland on three sides. The population of Maryland is more than 5.7 million.

Pages 8–9

In September 1814, the Battle of Baltimore was fought between American and British forces. Francis Scott Key, a lawyer from Maryland, boarded a British ship to negotiate the release of American prisoners. There, Key watched as British ships shelled Fort McHenry. At dawn, he saw the American flag still flying. Inspired by this, he wrote "The Star Spangled Banner."

Pages 10–11

The black-eyed susan is part of the sunflower family. It grows wild in Maryland. The farmer and the fisherman on the state seal hold a shield. It has the coat of arms of two families, the Calverts and the Crosslands. These two families helped settle the state in the 1630s.

Pages 12–13

The flag features the Maryland coat of arms, which is also seen on the state seal. The red and white part of the flag represents the Crossland family crest. The black and yellow part of the flag symbolizes the Calvert family crest. Black and yellow features in many Maryland symbols, including its state flower, bird, and insect.

Pages 14–15

The Baltimore oriole was named for George Calvert, who became Lord Baltimore. The oriole looks for caterpillars and other bugs on the bark and leaves of trees. The oriole's nest looks like a pouch hanging at the end of a branch. Baltimore's major league baseball team is named the Baltimore Orioles.

Pages 16–17

In 1649, colonists founded a settlement named Providence. Later, it was named Annapolis for Princess Anne of Great Britain, who became queen in the early 1700s. The U.S. Naval Academy opened in Annapolis in 1845 with a class of 50 midshipmen. Officers of the Navy and Marine Corps are still trained there today.

Pages 18–19

Blue crabs are said to be among the sweetest tasting crabs. Male blue crabs have blue claws, and females have red-tipped claws. Half of all blue crabs fished in the Unites States come from Chesapeake Bay. More than 460 million blue crabs live in Chesapeake Bay. Blue crab fishing contributes about $76 million to the Maryland economy each year.

Pages 20–21

Maryland's Chesapeake Bay is a place many tourists visit in the summer. It is the largest body of water in the state. People enjoy beachcombing, sailing, and fishing along the bay. Many people see the sights of Maryland from harbor cruises, sailboats, and water taxis.

KEY WORDS

Research has shown that as much as 65 percent of all written material published in English is made up of 300 words. These 300 words cannot be taught using pictures or learned by sounding them out. They must be recognized by sight. This book contains 50 common sight words to help young readers improve their reading fluency and comprehension. This book also teaches young readers several important content words, such as proper nouns. These words are paired with pictures to aid in learning and improve understanding.

Page	Sight Words First Appearance
4	a, group, is, it, of, line, old, the, state, this, was
7	four, in, next, part, to, where
11	and, can, feet, grow, has, left, man, men, on, right, two, up
12	come, from, white
15	eats, makes, sounds, when
16	city, named
19	are, each, live, more, than, water, year
20	different, kinds, many, mountains, people

Page	Content Words First Appearance
4	Maryland, soldiers
7	Atlantic Ocean, shape, United States
8	anthem, battle, Star Spangled Banner
11	black-eyed susan, crown, fisherman, flower, miner, seal
12	flag, families, patterns
15	bird, fruit, insects, nectar, oriole
16	Annapolis, capital, United States Naval Academy
19	bay, blue crabs, Chesapeake Bay, pounds
20	boats

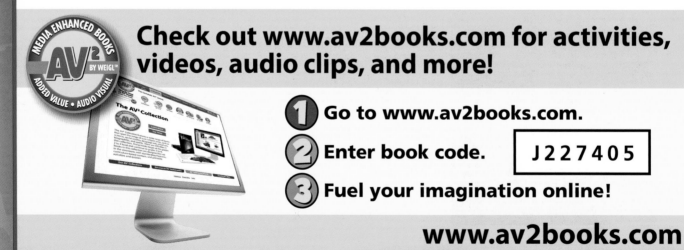